when...

answering your **TOUGHEST**
questions about
Sex, Love,
and Dating

by kevin moore

Harrison House
Tulsa, Oklahoma

16 15 14 13   7 6 5 4 3

What Do I Do When?
Answering Your Toughest Questions About Sex, Love, and Dating
ISBN 13: 978-1-57794-961-9
ISBN 10: 1-57794-961-7
Copyright © 2009 by Kevin Moore
P.O. Box 692032
Tulsa, Oklahoma 74169-2032

Published by Harrison House Publishers
P.O. Box 35035
Tulsa, Oklahoma 74135
www.harrisonhouse.com

Table of Contents

Introduction

Everybody has questions about sex, love, and dating, but sometimes it can feel really awkward to ask those questions. Whether you're at a stage when your parents won't let you date, you've just gotten asked out on your first date, or you're already really tight with your boyfriend or girlfriend, no matter where you are on the dating highway, one thing is for sure, you have questions.

Dating can be a lot of fun, but it can also be a battleground where a lot of people get hurt. From breakups to rebounds to broken hearts, dating can feel like one wild roller coaster ride.

So whether you're about to get on the dating roller coaster, or you're already enjoying it, I've written this book for you. Now, I'll probably not hit on all the questions you have about sex, love, and dating, but for the ones I do, I sure hope this helps.

May *His* best be yours,
—Kevin Moore

What Do I
Do When...

My Parents
Won't Let
Me Date?

It was an amazing moment. You were sitting in science class. The teacher was talking about the molecular structure of a cell, and you were totally bored out of your mind—when all of a sudden, it happened.

You glanced across the room and saw that special someone. Your eyes met. Sparks flew. Right away, you knew, *This is the one.* At the end of class, you jumped up from your seat and walked toward *the one.* You were on a mission. You could not wait to ask this person to join you Friday night for a movie and a romantic dinner at Taco Bell. It would be a date like no other.

Then it hit you.

You're not allowed to date. Your parents won't let you. What do you do now? You're crazy about this person. This person's crazy about you, but you can't even go out on a date. Now what do you do?

Relax

If your parents won't let you date, the first thing you have to do is relax. I know that's the last thing you want to do right now, but trust me—it's the right thing. Not being able to date is a lot like not being able to drive. You look around, and it seems like everyone and their brother is jumping in the car, racing down the highway, and having a great time—and you can't wait to join them. Don't worry. You will.

The Bible says in Ecclesiastes 3 that there is a time and a season for everything under the sun. Your time will come. You'll eventually go out with that person, and it will be amazing. But until then, relax.

Don't Treat Your Parents Like the Enemy

If your parents won't let you date, the second thing you need to do is to avoid treating them like the enemy. At first glance, this may seem like a crazy idea. I mean, after all, your parents are the ones not letting you go out on a date, right? So if they're not the enemy in this thing, who is?

Well, I agree it does sound a little strange. However, follow me on this one. Let's say, by some strange miracle, you were allowed to go out on a date tomorrow night. Who would you get the cash from to pay for the date? Well, unless you have a job, most likely you would get the money from your parents. Let's say that God miraculously moved on your behalf and your parents gave you permission to take your significant other out for dinner and a movie. If you can't drive, who's going to pick up your date and drop you both off at the movie theatre? Most likely, it would be your parents. If you can drive, who are you going to get the car keys from? Most likely, once again, it would be your folks.

You see, even though they are the ones not allowing you to go out on a date right now, it is important for you to realize that your parents are not your enemy. They are actually your friends. Eventually they will be the ones to not only give you permission to date, but also money and maybe even a car to go out and have a good time with someone you care about.

So before you start down the dating highway, it's important for you to clearly understand that God has given your parents to you not to hurt, but to help. Don't treat them like enemies who are out to get you. Treat them like friends who will be a great asset to you in the future.

Here are some tips on how to do just that.

1. Let Your Parents Give You Some Advice

To treat your parents like friends, the first thing you need to do is to let them give you some advice. Whether you like it or not, your parents are a part of your life. And whether you know it or not, they want to be a part of your life. So let them.

Proverbs 1:8 says, "Listen, my son, to your father's instruction and do not forsake your mother's teaching." God tells you to listen to your parents' advice. The reason is that your parents were once right where you are. Now, I know it was probably back when dinosaurs roamed the Earth, but even still, they have already experienced the

same things you're experiencing, and—believe it or not—
they probably have some good information to give you.

God has given you your parents to help guide and direct
you through every phase of your life. So let them.

2. Don't Buck the System

To treat your parents like friends, you can't buck the
system. A lot of times, it's easy for us to think our parents' sole purpose for existing on planet Earth is to do
nothing but ruin our lives. That's why they give us all
these rules and regulations to keep us from doing what
we want to do, like date. However, that couldn't be
further from the truth.

Your parents love you and they feel like the rules they have
laid out for you are in your best interest. Whether you
agree or disagree with their rules, it's important that you
don't buck the system.

Jesus says in Luke 16:10, "Whoever can be trusted with
very little can also be trusted with much, and whoever is
dishonest with very little will also be dishonest with much."

Before your parents will allow you to do more, they have to
know they can trust you. The best way to get your parents
to trust you is not to break the rules, but to obey them.

Don't do things under the table or on the sly. If you cannot
prove to your parents they can trust you with what they've

given to you now, they will never trust you when it comes to something more—like dating.

So here's the bottom line. What are your parents' current rules for you when it comes to dating or crushing on someone? Whatever they are, follow them to a T. Don't bend the rules. Don't break the rules or try and hide things from your parents. Prove to your parents they can trust you, and eventually they will give you more.

Discover Who You Are, Not Who You Want

If your parents won't let you date, you need to use this time to discover who you are rather than who you want. A mistake a lot of people make is letting the person they like determine who they are. If a girl likes a guy who's into sports, then the girl gets into sports. If a guy likes a girl who's into movies, all of a sudden he becomes a movie specialist.

This seems harmless enough. But it's actually very dangerous, because if who you are is only determined by the person you are with, then what if there comes a day when you are not with that person anymore? Who are you then?

Here are a few things you can begin to do that will help you discover who you are, what you like, and what you want to do with your life.

1. Excel in a Sport

   If you want to discover who you are, get out there on a
   sports team or into an individual sport and excel in it.
   Don't just join a team or play a sport. Excel in it. Show up
   early for practice and leave late. Start a workout regimen
   and change your diet to help sculpt and shape your body
   for better performance. Take the next few months to
   become the best you possibly can at the sport you have
   chosen to play.

2. Start Playing an Instrument

   If you want to discover who you are, pick up an instrument. Talk to your parents and ask to take some guitar,
   piano, or drum lessons after school. It's a great way to
   meet some new and interesting people, as well as possibly discovering a talent you never knew you had.

3. Volunteer

   To discover who you are, try volunteering. We all want to
   make a difference. So make one. Find a place in your
   school, church youth group or children's ministry to use
   your talents and abilities to make a positive impact in the
   world around you.

4. Get a Part-Time Job

   To discover who you are, check out options for a part-
   time job. You don't have to wait until you're older to start

making cash. Take on a paper route, start a lawn mowing business, work at a summer camp, or talk to your parents about working for them around the house or doing yard work every week. Find something that you love to do, and do it so well that people will pay you to do it.

Read the Bible Every Day

If your parents won't let you date right now, the fourth thing you need to do is read the Bible every day. The Bible is more than just something to read when you're in church or to turn to when you get into trouble. Take the next few months to get into the habit of reading God's Word every day. The more you read and learn about God, the more you will discover about yourself.

I know you can't wait for your parents to throw you the keys to the car and let you start driving down the dating highway. But until that day comes, relax, don't treat them like the enemy, and discover who you are rather than who you want. When the time finally comes and you start dating, you'll be glad you did.

What Do I
Do When...

I Like
Someone
Who Doesn't
Know I Exist?

I was about ten years old, and it was a blistering hot day. I had spent my entire morning riding my bike and playing basketball with some friends. The bowl of Lucky Charms® I'd eaten for breakfast had long since worn off, and I was starving. My grandma was making lunch in less than a half hour, but I couldn't wait that long. I was desperate. I needed some food, and I needed it quick.

So I went to the kitchen, and on Grandma's counter I saw a huge bowl of vanilla ice cream just sitting there waiting for someone to eat it. I grabbed a spoon, scooped up a mountain of ice cream, and shoved it in my mouth. It was at that point that I came to the shocking realization that what I had just shoveled in my mouth was not ice cream.

It was lard.

That's right. Bacon grease. Pig fat. Call it whatever you want, but it was disgusting.

I will never forget that day—and even worse, I will never forget that taste. I was so hungry; I was so desperate that I did whatever I had to do to get some food. Big mistake.

So with that story in mind, what do you do when you like someone but they don't know you exist? It's pretty simple, really: don't get desperate.

I'm not sure why, but when we're trying to get someone to notice us and it's not working, it's very easy for us to get into desperate mode. This is a big mistake because every time we get desperate, we never get what we really want.

Telltale Signs That You're Desperate

Here are two telltale signs that you are desperate.

1. ## You Do Anything To Get Their Attention

   The first indication that you're desperate is that you'll do anything to get this person's attention.

   Guys, here's the deal. Girls want a guy who has some self-confidence. Someone who knows who he is and what he stands for. When you act the fool or over the top all the time, you come across as unstable and insecure, and insecurity is not a quality that young ladies find attractive.

   Girls, you need to understand that guys are hunters by nature and are always up for a chase. When you go gaga over some guy and let him know you are crazy about him, you've just told him that the chase is over and he totally has you. Because he has you, he will naturally start over-looking you and start chasing someone he doesn't have.

   If you like somebody and want him or her to notice you, instead of doing a bunch of crazy stuff, just be yourself. Walk up to your crush, say, "Hello," and then walk away or maybe hang out with the group at a ball game for a few minutes—but just be yourself. When you become so desperate that you will do anything to get the attention of the one you like, you become pretty easy to ignore.

2. You Willingly Become Something You Aren't

The second telltale sign that you're desperate is that you willingly become something you aren't when you're around this person.

I knew a girl who always had to have a boyfriend. Every few months, she'd come to church with a new guy. I started to notice that, besides the fact that they were all pretty sharp-looking, each of these guys was totally different.

One guy was an athlete. He was big, strong, and had a letter jacket. You could tell he was a beast on the football field. Well, it wasn't long before they broke up.

A few weeks later, she showed up at church with another guy. This dude was totally different from the first. He was really tall and skinny. He wasn't into sports at all. He was into music, drama, and the arts. He was pretty cool but, alas, that relationship crashed and burned as well.

Not too long after the breakup, she showed up with yet another guy. He was entirely different than the other two. He wasn't into sports or the arts. He was into grunge rock and parties. That relationship fizzled out quickly as well.

Observing this revolving door of dead-end dating, I started to notice something about the young lady. Every time she was with a guy, she morphed into someone exactly like each one.

When she was dating the athlete, she was all about sports. She wore his letter jacket. She went to every ball game. She was always talking about football. She was a sports junky.

But when that relationship ended and she started dating the artsy guy, she stopped talking about sports and started talking about more cultural things. She even changed her hair and the way she dressed.

When that relationship ended and she started going out with the rocker, she dropped the modern clothes and classical talk and started going for things with a little harder edge.

With each relationship that she wanted to have, she became something she wasn't just to please the guy she was with. She thought that if she would become what she thought he wanted her to be, he would love her and want to be part of her life.

She was wrong.

When it comes to gaining the affection and attention of others, one thing you need to keep in mind is that people don't want you to be what you think they want you to be. They want you to be yourself. If you have to become something you aren't just to get someone's attention or affection, it won't work. The person won't like you for long, and eventually you won't like yourself all that much either.

When it comes to getting someone else's attention, the best advice I can give is to just be yourself. Let a potential relationship grow up out of who you are, not who you think they want you to be.

Better Patient Than Desperate

When you've got someone you're crazy about and the person isn't even giving you the time of day, it's very easy to get desperate and do anything to get the person to like you—but don't. Don't get desperate. Be patient.

On that fateful day when I ate lard, all I would have had to do was wait thirty minutes, and my grandma would have made me a great lunch that would have been a lot better than the pig fat I shoved in my face.

It's the same with you. Scripture teaches us that we should be patient and wait on God to move on our behalf. (See Isa. 40:31.) You may or may not know it, but God has your back. He's looking out for you, and if you will not get desperate, if you'll be patient, and if you'll just be yourself, at just the right moment God will bring the right person into your life. It may not be who you think it will be, and it may take longer than what you thought it would take. But trust me on this one—it's better to be patient than to be desperate.

What Do I
Do When...

I Have
a Date?

It finally happened. The question was asked. The answer was given. The details were arranged. Congratulations! You have a date! What do you do now?

Well, here are just a few things to keep in mind as you prepare for your date.

Set Some Boundaries

Once you get a date, the first thing you need to do is to set some boundaries. I said earlier that dating is a lot like driving. A lot of people drive down the dating highway with no idea where they're going, no idea of rules, and no idea of speed limits. They just jump in the car, throw caution to the wind, and go, go, go. They have the misconception that living life with no rules or guidelines will help them have a great dating experience. However, that is not how God set it up.

Take a look at what the Bible says in James 1:25: "The man [or woman, or teenage girl or boy] who looks intently into the perfect law that gives freedom, and continues to do this, not forgetting what he [or she] has heard, but doing it—he [or she] will be blessed in what he [or she] does."

God will bless everything you do if you obey the perfect law that sets you free. What sets us free to enjoy life to its fullest is not doing whatever we want whenever we want; rather, what sets us free are rules and boundaries. This goes against everything you think and feel, but if you want to have the real connection you're looking for in your dating relationship, you have to set up some boundaries.

Habakkuk 2:2 says, "Then the LORD replied: 'Write down the revelation and make it plain on tablets so that a herald may run with it.'" Before you get too far down this dating road, you need to sit down and think about what rules and boundaries you're going to let guide your dating life. Once you know what they are, write them down. Put them in a place where you'll see them every day, and maybe even sit down with your parents and let them know your dating plan. Here is an example.

My Dating Boundaries

- we can hang out together (games, movies, etc.)

- we can hold hands

- we can put arms around each other

- we can talk on the phone and text

- we cannot have prolonged alone time

- we cannot stay out together past 11:00

- we will not engage in intimate kissing or touching

Get To Know the Person, Not the Body

··

Okay, you've got a date. Chances are you think this person is pretty hot or you would not be going out together. So we have the physical attraction thing down. But how do you match up with this person otherwise? The only way to find out is to put yourself in situations where you can actually get to know this person, not just his or her body.

Here are two ways to get to know your date personally.

1. Date in Groups

Dating in groups is one of the best ways to actually get to know someone.

Think about it. When you go out one on one, all you see is what the other person wants you to see: his or her best smile, best hair, best clothes and best behavior. You don't really get to know the real person until at least the third or fourth date.

However, if you'll start off dating in groups, you'll see the person for who he or she really is. You'll see how this person interacts with friends and what his or her sense of humor is really like. Plus, being around several people you know kind of takes the edge off the night and makes it a lot less awkward than it is when it's just you and your date.

I know dating in groups may sound kind of old school, but give it a try. I think you'll like it.

2. Do Things That Cause You To Talk

The second way to get to know your date personally is to do things that cause you to talk. The purpose of dating is having a good time while getting to know someone you're interested in. Right? If that's the case, then why do most dates consist of sitting in a dark movie theater staring at a giant screen beside the person we want to get to know but can't talk to because it would be rude to the people around us?

Now, there's nothing inherently wrong with going to dinner and a movie. However, don't make that your weekly date. Here are some options that are a lot of fun as well.

Go bowling. Yep, bowling. Nothing spells date night excitement like trying to look cool while rolling a black rock toward some white pins.

Play putt-putt. Get to know your date while trying to hit a ball through a giant, turning windmill. It takes no athletic ability, and it makes for great conversation.

Host a game night. Invite a few of your and your date's best friends to your house for board games, pizza, and some movies. Even if your date turns out to be not so cool, you'll still have a great time hanging with your buds.

Go to the mall. Pick up your date, and go to the mall. After browsing the aisles of each of your favorite stores, head to the food court and get to know each other while sharing a smoothie.

Go out to eat at a hibachi grill. Watching some dude chop up your food over a flaming skillet is a great way to spend a Friday night with your special someone. The food is great, and if you pick the right friends to join you, this could be a night to remember.

Keep "I love you" Out of Your Romantic Vocabulary

The third thing to do when you've got a date is to remember to keep "I love you" out of the conversation.

Okay, here's how it normally works. David and Susie like each other, but neither one knows how the other feels. Susie decides to break the silence and take the first step. So she sends a messenger to let David know exactly how she feels. Now, normally a messenger is someone who cannot get a date him- or herself but wants to be involved in the dating process somehow, so this person becomes a messenger.

The messenger comes up and says to David, "Did you know Susie likes you?"

David then replies, "Well, no I did not know that. However, that's interesting because I like Susie, too."

The messenger then returns to Susie with the good news, and from that time on David and Susie are dating. He's committed to her, and she's committed to him.

After a few months of going out, David gets up enough courage to let Susie know how he feels so he says the three words that melt every girls heart, "I love you."

Shocked and elated that David is so open about his feelings, Susie quickly replies, "I love you, too."

Now it's on. *I love you's* start flying anywhere and everywhere. Talking on the phone, e-mails, and text messages are all filled with *I love you*. During social studies class when the teacher isn't looking, Susie looks David's way, blows him a kiss, and uses sign language to spell out *I love you*. David catches the kiss and signs back the amazingly romantic words Susie can't wait to hear.

From the outside looking in, this seems so innocent, so normal, so nice. But it's not.

The problem with *I love you* being a vital part of your dating vocabulary is that in American society and dating culture "love" and "sex" (or physical intimacy) are practically interchangeable. Because of this, the three words that everyone wants to hear often pull people down a road of intimacy that they're not ready for.

Ecclesiastes 3:1 says, "There is a time for everything, and a season for every activity under heaven." There will be a time for *I love you*, but dating is not that time.

The more you say, "I love you," to the person you're dating, the more you'll become convinced that *kissy kissy*, *huggy huggy*, and *touchy touchy* are totally acceptable things to do. *After all*, you'll tell yourself, *that's what people who love each other do. Right?* Wrong.

You see, *kissy kissy*, *huggy huggy*, and *touchy touchy* (and I think you know what I mean by that) is what married people do. Right now you are dating, but you are not married.

There is a time and a place for everything. Even though you have strong feelings for this person, as much as possible, keep *I love you* out of your romantic vocabulary until you are either giving or receiving a ring. In the long run, you and your date will be glad you did.

Remember: You're Dating; You're Not Married

The fourth thing to do when you've got a date is to remember you're dating; you're not married. Do you know of a couple who are dating, but might as well be married? Every day they drive home from school together. They do their homework together. They eat together. They even go to family functions together.

People who are tied to the ball and chain of "always together" usually say things like this: "Girls, I'd love to go to the mall with you, but I can't because I've got to be one of the four people to watch Shawn wrestle." Or "Listen guys, I want to go to the game, but I can't because I'm going to Debby's piano recital." Or "Dude, you guys are going paint balling? I'd love to go, but my girlfriend's cousin's uncle's friend died and I'm going to the funeral."

What? This isn't dating. This is marriage.

Too many dating teenagers spend an awful lot of time acting like they're married. They're always together. As you're starting your dating relationship, make sure you're not one of them.

It seems very normal to always want to be with your crush; however, it can be dangerous, and here's why: Privacy demands intimacy.

The more you're together, the more intimate you become. The more intimate you become, the more married you feel. The more married you feel, the more married activities you will get involved in.

You'll start to reason that if you'll one day get married anyway, you might as well get on with getting on with it. So you'll push on the physical accelerator and go too far, too fast. After the break up (and there's like a 90 percent chance there will be one), you'll be left emotionally and sexually stranded on the side of the road. That is not where God wants you to be.

Now, am I saying that you should never under any circumstances be alone with your date? Am I saying that if you ever get together more than one time a week you'll become sexually active and ruin your life? No, not necessarily.

What I'm saying is you're not married, so don't act like it. Don't be afraid to undo the chain and take a break once in a while. I know it can be tough, but for you and your date's spiritual, emotional, and physical well-being, it would be a good idea to be wise about how much time you spend together, especially alone.

What Do I
Do When...

I Think I'm
in Love?

There was a guy in the Bible you've probably heard a little bit about; his name was Samson. Now, Samson is best known for getting a bad haircut from his girlfriend, Delilah, but I want to address something that went down years before all of that.

Here's the deal. One day, Samson went to a Philistine town called Timnah. While he was there, he saw this smoking hot babe who stole his heart the very first time he laid eyes on her. Samson was blown away by this girl. As soon as he saw her, he ran back to his house and told his father he'd seen his future wife and wanted to marry her. (See Judges 14:1,2.)

Now, stop and think about this for a minute. Samson sees the girl for the very first time, and his first inclination is not to talk to her, not to ask her out, not to get to know her a little bit. No, the very first thing Samson wants to do is marry her. After seeing her only once, he wants to make a lifelong commitment to this woman he doesn't even know.

May I be bold enough to say *that's crazy*? Samson saw someone he wanted, and he was on such a high that he let his emotions lead him to a hasty decision that he never should have made.

We need to look no further than the story of Samson to find the answer to the question, "What do I do when I think I'm in love?"

Proceed With Caution

If you think you're in love, the first thing you need to do is proceed with caution. If you look at the entirety of Samson's life, there was no such thing as caution with him. He was constantly letting his emotions lead him to making decisions without really thinking them through. This was a big mistake. A hasty decision led Samson to marry this girl he would later leave.

If you have someone you have strong feelings for, that's great. However, never let those feelings be the deciding factor on what you will and will not do. Proverbs 21:5 says, "The plans of the diligent lead to profit as surely as haste leads to poverty."

If you've been dating someone for a while and you think you're in love, my advice is to proceed with caution. Don't let your emotions lead you to hasty decisions. Learn a valuable lesson from Samson: Slow down and think things through before you do something you might later regret.

Give Your Date Some Space

If you think you're in love, the second thing you need to do is give your date some space. When my family and I first moved to Tulsa, I was introduced to an authentic Mexican restaurant. It was incredible. The burritos, the enchiladas, the fajitas, and the chips and salsa were unlike anything I had ever eaten before. I was hooked. I went through a phase when I ate there at least once a week. I was in love with this restaurant.

However, a funny thing started to happen. About four weeks into my affair with this Mexican restaurant, I started to not enjoy it as much. Now, I would still go there and eat because it was what I always did. I would order the same thing every time, but not because I really wanted it; it was just what I always ate. Eventually I was pretty bored and stopped going there altogether.

It's the same with you and the person you're dating. When you first start going out, it's incredible. The feelings, the emotions—you are in love.

Because of this, you start doing everything together. School, homework, and holidays—you're always together. You text each other at least fifty-three times every single day. You talk on the phone for hours at a time. It's incredible.

But just like anything else, if you don't give it a break from time to time, you might burn out. Oh, you may still get together all the time and text like machines. But like me and my Mexican restaurant, you or your date may keep doing all the stuff you've always done, but out of habit and not out of love.

So this is my advice: If you really love this person, give him or her some space. Go out with your friends without your date for a weekend or two. Let his or her family eat dinner without you at the table. I know it sounds strange, but they did have dinners together before you were ever part of their lives.

I don't know all the things you and your date could change, but this weekend sit down with your date and talk openly and honestly about how much time you're spending together and what might need to change. Find ways to give each other some space, and let your relationship breathe a little bit. If you do, I think you will both be glad you did.

Enjoy the Moment

If you think you're in love, the third thing you need to do is enjoy the moment. If you knew that you only had one year to live, what would that year be like? Think about how differently you would treat every day. Every moment you lived would be a miracle. You would live every second of every day to its absolute fullest. Knowing you could not plan for the future would make you enjoy each moment even more.

Right now you have someone you feel really strongly about. You've probably been going out for a while. There's probably a real connection between the two of you. In fact, you may feel so strongly for this person that you think you're in love.

You know what? That's great. I'm really happy for you. But in answering the question "What do I do when I think I'm in love?" I have to be totally honest with you as well. The truth of the matter is that, if percentages are correct, most likely this relationship only has about one year to live. I know this may be a real shocker, but there's a very strong chance that the relationship you're in right now will not make it all the way to marriage.

Most likely, the feelings and emotions you have for this person will at some point change, and your dating relationship will end. So make up your mind to enjoy each moment to its absolute fullest. Go out, have fun, talk, laugh, and learn from each other. Knowing that this probably won't last forever doesn't have to be a huge downer. In fact, it can actually allow you to enjoy what you have together even more.

Dangers of Making Long-Term Plans

Here are some dangers in making long-term plans right now.

1. ## Getting the Physical Party Started Too Early

   The first risk of making long-term plans is that you could get the physical party started too early. You know it's true. The longer you're together, the more you're alone. The more you're alone, the harder and harder it gets to keep your hands to yourself and not get physical with the person you care about.

2. Getting Distracted From What You Need To Do

The second risk of making long-term plans is that you could get distracted from what you need to do. There are only so many minutes in each day. The more time you spend with your significant other, the more your calendar gets jam-packed with his or her activities. That's great and no big deal at all—when you're married. But remember: You're not married; you are dating. What about your life? What about your schedule? What about the things you want to do? A true match made in heaven will add to, and not take away from, the goals you have as an individual.

3. Missing Out on Who God Has for You

The third risk of making long-term plans is that you may miss out on who God has for you. I constantly hear people say, "If I don't explore this relationship for all it could be, I may miss out on the person God has for me." I guess, in a way, that could be true. But it could also be true that if you *do* explore this relationship for all it could be, you may miss out on the person God has for you.

When I look at my life and the different people I dated in the past, and then look at my life now and the amazing wife I've been married to for seventeen years, I know for a fact that if I would have explored any of the previous relationships for all they could have been, I would have missed out on the person God, the Creator of the universe, had personally handpicked and created to be my wife.

Over the next few years, enjoy each moment. But don't make long-range plans with the person you're with. Let God be God. I know from experience He has your back.

Am I trying to be Billy Bummer on your dating life? No, not really. But the honest truth is that from the ages of twelve to twenty, who you are is changing every single day—and who you are determines who you want. If who you are is constantly changing over the next few years, it only stands to reason that who you want will change as well.

If You're in Love

What do you do when you think you're in love? Proceed with caution, give your date some space, enjoy each moment, and don't plan long-range. Who knows? You may end up marrying this person and having the perfect life together. However, you'll both be a lot better off if, right now anyway, you don't plan on it.

What Do I
Do When...

My Date
Wants
To Get
Physical?

Have you ever wanted something really, really badly? I don't mean *kind* of wanted it. I'm talking you want it so badly you'll do anything and everything you can to try to get it.

I was like that once. I was about twelve years old, and I played on my church basketball team. We were a ragtag team of short kids who couldn't play basketball to save our lives, but we looked great in our burnt orange jerseys with black lettering.

All that year, I heard that if you got picked for the all-star team you would get to play in Market Square Arena, where the Pacers used to play.

Only one person from each team got to be on the all-star team, and I desperately wanted that person to be me. I did push-ups. I did sit-ups. I ran extra "down and backs" at practice. After school every day, I would shoot baskets for hours at my Uncle Jim's house. Man, I wanted to get picked for the all-star team and play on an actual professional basketball court.

We only won a few games that entire year. However, I actually didn't play that badly. I started every game, scored a lot of baskets, and also got a ton of rebounds. By the end of the season, the top two choices for the all-star team were me and my best friend, Troy Pratt.

I wanted to be an all star so badly I could taste it. I remember sitting in my classroom at school daydreaming about stealing the ball, driving the length of the court, and laying the ball up and in for a basket. I imagined myself in my short shorts and knee-high tube socks running down the court in Market Square Arena.

Well, the day finally came when coach would let us know who made the all-star team. I was totally sick to my stomach all day, but as I walked into the gym that night, I just knew I was going to be the one picked.

But it didn't happen. I didn't make the all-star team that year. Troy did.

I was devastated. To this day, I remember sitting at Market Square Arena watching Troy play in the all-star game, thinking the whole time, *It should have been me.*

You may be reading this story and wondering, *What in the world does a twelve-year-old boy in short shorts and 1970s tube socks who wanted to be on an all-star team have to do with answering my question "What do I do when my date wants to get physical?"* Well, I guess the moral of the story is this: *You don't always get what you want.*

And you know what? Those seven words are exactly what your date needs to hear you say the next time he or she tries to get what he or she wants from you.

Everybody always wants something. If the something your date is wanting from you has anything to do with *huggy,*

huggy, kissy, kissy, or *touchy touchy,* here are a few things you need to do.

Draw A Line in the Sand

When your date wants to get physical, the first thing you personally have to do is draw a line in the sand. Romans 6:13 says, "Do not offer the parts of your body to sin, as instruments of wickedness, but rather offer yourselves to God, as those who have been brought from death to life; and offer the parts of your body to him as instruments of righteousness."

The bottom line is that your body is 100 percent yours. You set the tone for what you will and will not do with it. Long before your date wants to get physical, you as an individual have to draw a line in the sand to clearly define for yourself where your physical boundary line actually is.

Where Exactly Is the Line?

Now, this brings up the age-old and often asked question of *How far is too far?* I think there are three things you need to do in order to know how far is too far.

1. The Grandparents Test

   First of all, to discover where the line is, take the grandparents test. Ask yourself one simple question: *Would I feel comfortable doing this in front of my grandma and grandpa?* That's right. Your grandma and grandpa. Would you feel comfortable sucking face in front of your grandpa? Would you feel comfortable letting your significant other's hands roam all over your body while your granny is right there in front of you knitting a sweater for her cat?

No?

Well then, that's where you need to draw the line. Whatever you would not feel comfortable doing with your grandma and grandpa watching from the living room couch, would be too far.

2. Check the Bible

Second, to discover where the line is, check the Bible. In order to know where your line should be, the second thing you need to do is look at what Scripture teaches. There are many biblical texts on sexual purity in the Bible. In fact, here's a great verse to start with: "Flee from sexual immorality. All other sins a man commits are outside his body, but he who sins sexually sins against his own body" (1 Cor. 6:18).

God instructs us to flee, to run away from, anything that is sexually immoral. So that gives you a good idea of where your line should be. Basically, your line should not be anywhere near anything a married couple would do when they are having sex. I don't think I need to get too graphic here; I'm sure you are more than able to draw your own conclusions.

3. Get Some Good Advice

The third and final thing you need to do is get some good advice. The Bible says, "many advisers make victory sure" (Prov. 11:14).

One of the best places you can go for advice on drawing your line is to your parents. I'm sure you just cringed at the thought of having another sex talk with your folks. I mean, it was awkward enough the first time. Right?

Well, the truth is that even though it might be awkward, God has given your parents to you to help you with some of your big decisions. They've already been where you are, and believe it or not, they have your best interest in mind.

So before your date has a chance to try and push you to your physical limit, give yourself the grandparents test, look at what the Bible says, and have a heart to heart with your mom and dad. Doing these three things will help you know exactly where your line should be.

Let Them Know Where Your Line Is

When you start going out and your date wants to get physical, the second thing you need to do is let the other person know right away where your line is. To do this, you don't have to hand all of your dates a three-page legal document that clearly states what you will and will not allow them to do to your physical person. That would be very weird, and I'm sure your date would be over rather quickly, as well.

Don't Get Close to the Line

No, it doesn't have to be a written document, and it doesn't have to be weird. You can let your date know where your line is, first of all, by not allowing him or her to get anywhere near the line.

If your line stops at holding hands, then don't let your date physically turn the corner and start driving sixty miles an hour toward Make Out City. If you let someone get started toward the line and then tell him or her to stop, you are sending mixed signals. Your date may be nice and stop this time, but trust me—all the way home, your date will be thinking about driving you further down the physical highway next time you're together. The best thing to do in these situations is to not let your date get anywhere close to where your physical finish line begins.

Talk About It

Second, if you've been dating for a while, you can let your significant other know where your line is by talking about it.

Actually sit down and say, "These are my standards, here's why I have them, and if you want to be with me you need to not only abide by these standards but also agree with them."

Your date agreeing with your standards is very important to the life of your relationship because Scripture teaches us in Amos 3:3, "Do two walk together unless they have agreed to do so?" When it comes to where you will and will not go physically, if you and your date want to go in two different directions, there's no way you can truly walk together. Either you will go your separate ways, or one of you will give in to the other.

I've found that usually the one to give in to the other person is not the one with the high standards. More times than not, the teenager who has good, godly standards but continues to date someone who's trying to get physical begins to slowly compromise and lower his or her standards in order to please the other. This is a huge mistake.

Draw your line in the sand. Let your date know where your line is, and if he or she crosses your line, even once, move on.

Move On

When your date wants to get physical, and you've done everything you can to uphold your standards but your date is still pushing you, it's time to move on. There are only a few things in life that you only have one of, and your body is one of them.

If your date, the person who says he or she cares about you, doesn't respect your wishes when it comes to your one and only body and how it's treated, then move on.

I know. I'm sure you had a real heart to heart and your date apologized, but move on. I know your date promised it will never happen again, but move on. I know your date agreed with your standards, and this was just a one-time moment of weakness on both of your parts, but move on.

You see, physical touches are a lot like potato chips. Once you have one, you've got to go back and get some more. I'm sure this person likes you. I'm sure this person is sorry, but he or she will be back for more. Did you play a part in the first mistake? Absolutely, you did. You compromised once and you could compromise again, so this person will be back for more.

Only One Life

So what do you do when your date wants to get physical? Draw a line in the sand. Let them know where your line is. And if they cross the line, move on. I know it's a lot easier for me to say than it is for you to do, but remember: you only have one life and one body. Don't waste either of them on someone who doesn't care about you enough to respect your wishes.

What Do I
Do When...

I've Gone
Too Far?

The last few times you'd gone out, things had started heating up. You hadn't done anything you felt guilty for, but with every date you'd definitely been creeping closer and closer to the magic line that you'd said you wouldn't cross.

Even though you knew you were getting into some dangerous territory, it was fun. It was exciting. It was really cool that someone was giving you that much attention. There wasn't really a problem; you knew you just needed to be careful.

Then it happened. You weren't planning on it, but you were alone. One thing led to another, and before you knew it, you'd gone too far.

What do you do now?

Repent of the Sin

In our politically correct culture, it's easy for us to change the names of things we don't like simply because they come across as negative and harsh. Because of this, it would be very easy for me to say the first thing you need to do when you've gone too far is to admit you "made a mistake" or maybe apologize for the "rash decision" you made in a moment of weakness. However, the truth of the matter is that when you made the decision to cross the line sexually with someone you were not married to, you did not just "make a mistake" or a "rash decision"; you fell short of God's standard. Plain and simply, you *sinned*.

I know that's not very PC, but it's true. When you've gone too far physically, the first thing you need to do is repent of your sin.

Sexual purity is God's standard. However, He knows you're not perfect. God is well aware that there may be times, in moments of weakness, when you fall short of the standard He has set for you. When this happens, He is more than willing to forgive you and wipe your slate clean, but you must first own up to what you've done.

The Bible tells us in 1 John 1:9, "If we confess our sins, he is faithful and just to forgive us our sins and purify us from all unrighteousness." When you openly *confess,* which means *to admit,* to God what you have done, you allow Him to forgive you and make you completely clean once again.

So if you've blown it, made a mistake, *sinned,* then today—in fact, maybe even right now—take the time to get alone somewhere and let God know all about what you've done. Own up to all of it. Apologize, *repent* (in other words, turn away from sin and toward God), and let Him completely forgive you.

Reject the Guilt

After you've repented, the next thing you need to do is reject the guilt. If you bought a video game that did not work, would you keep it in your PSP system for months, or would you take it back to the store? If you had just bought a pair of jeans and once you got them home you knew they were way too small, would you keep trying to squeeze into them, or would you take them back?

In both cases, wouldn't you return the item? Why would you send back a video game that doesn't work or get rid of a pair of jeans that do not fit? You would do it because they're of absolutely no use to you. Right?

It's the same with guilt. Guilt is not good; it's of no use to you, so why keep it around? A lot of people walk around carrying guilt for years. They did something they shouldn't have twenty years ago, but they still feel guilty for it today. To me, that's a lot like someone walking around with a video game in the PSP that doesn't work or wearing a pair of jeans that doesn't fit. It makes absolutely no sense.

If you've gone too far physically, repent of the sin and then reject (get rid of) the guilt.

Three Ways To Reject Guilt

Here are three ways to reject guilt.

1. Believe What God Says About You

The first way to reject guilt is to believe what God says about you. The Bible says, "Faith comes from hearing the message, and the message is heard through the word of

Christ" (Rom. 10:17). Here are some verses that will strengthen your faith in who you are in Christ.

Salvation

First, God says you are saved. First John 5:11-12 says, "And this is the testimony: God has given us eternal life, and this life is in his Son. He who has the Son has life; he who does not have the Son of God does not have life."

God lets us know in His Word that eternal life (salvation) can only be found through his Son, Jesus Christ. If you have accepted Jesus Christ as your Savior, then you are saved. The next time guilt tries to throw your past up to you, quote 1 John 5:11-12 and remind your guilt, as well as yourself, that through Christ you are a child of God.

Power Over Temptation

Second, God says you have power over temptation. First Corinthians 10:13 says, "No temptation has seized you except what is common to man. And God is faithful; he will not let you be tempted beyond what you can bear. But when you are tempted, he will also provide a way out so that you can stand up under it."

This Scripture is cool for two reasons.

First of all, it lets you know you're not alone. Everyone, and I do mean everyone, has gone through the same temptations that you are facing right now.

Second, it lets you know God is always faithful. Before the temptation ever comes, God has already made a way for you to escape it.

If you've messed up in the past, take a few minutes to think about the reasons why. Did you ignore some warning signs? Did you overlook some escape routes God was providing for you and your date?

The past is over and done with, so there is no need to dwell on it. Before the next temptation comes, realize you're not alone, and start asking God for ways you can avoid the next situation.

Forgiveness

Third, God says you are forgiven. First John 1:9 says, "If we confess our sins, he is faithful and just to forgive us our sins and purify us from all unrighteousness."

God is a good God, and He wants to forgive you. So ask.

Guidance

Fourth, God says He will guide you. Proverbs 3:5-6 says, "Trust in the LORD with all your heart and lean not on your own understanding; in all your ways acknowledge him, and he will make your paths straight."

Can't you see by now that God loves you? He tells you in His Word that He will save you, help you through tempting situations, forgive you if you mess up, and—if you will simply trust Him—lead you through the entire journey of your life.

You made a mistake, but that does not have to define you as a person. If you've gone too far recently, start speaking these four Scriptures over your life every single day. Every time the guilt from your past starts to creep in, speak the Word of God and begin to remind yourself how much God loves you and who you are in Him.

Stop Thinking About
What Happened

After you've repented and rejected the guilt, it's time to stop thinking about it. Did you know that your mind is like a giant filing cabinet? Every time you do something—it could be a big thing, small thing, good thing, or bad thing—it automatically gets filed away in the folders of your mind. So when you have blown it, it's very easy to go over to the cabinet, pull out the file, and replay it over and over again in your mind.

Every time you rewind in your mind, you begin to beat yourself up in your mind. You think, *Why in the world did I do that? I am so stupid. I will mess up again. It felt so good that I won't be able to say no next time either, so I might as well give up.*

Let me ask you a question. Who do you think these thoughts are coming from? Are they coming from God? No, they're coming from your enemy, the devil. He would like nothing more than for you to constantly feel guilty and never be able to truly let go of something that God has long since forgotten. So he tries to get you to think about what you did over and over again.

Here's the deal. You messed up, but you owned up to your mistake. You asked God to forgive you, and He did. So move on. Close the file cabinet, and stop thinking about something that has already been forgiven.

Stop Talking About What Happened

Not only do you need to repent of your sin, reject the guilt, and stop thinking about what happened, but you need to stop talking about it. Remember Uncle Rico from *Napoleon Dynamite*? That dude was jacked up, wasn't he? Besides the fact that he had a really sick van, he was constantly talking about what could have and should have been, back in the day. "If coach would've put me in fourth quarter, we would've been state champions. I'd have gone pro. I'd be soakin' it up in a hot tub with my soul mate." Uncle Rico was so verbally entrenched in the past that he wasn't able to enjoy the present.

Have you ever known somebody who had Uncle Rico syndrome? When it comes to your questionable past, it's easy to get caught up in Uncle Rico syndrome and talk to your date about the mistake you guys should've never made; to talk to your friends about the big "no no" you did a few weeks ago; to have private conversations with yourself about what you could have, should have, and wish you would have done differently on that fateful night. When this happens, just like good ol' Uncle Rico, you begin to live so much in the past that you cannot experience what God has for you today.

When you think about the past, instead of rehashing it, just ask God to forgive you. Then drop it. Stop talking about it. The bottom line is you messed up. It's over, so stop talking about it.

Remove the Problem

You've repented of your sin, rejected the guilt, and stopped thinking and talking about it. Now it's time to remove the problem.

I know this may sound gross, but I used to have a problem with my elbow bleeding. I know this is awfully sick, a bit personal, and certainly strange, but track along with me. When I was young, at least one time per week my elbow would start to bleed really badly. Now, the reason this would happen is that I had a huge wart on the end of my elbow and it was constantly getting scraped on something and busting open.

After about a month of washing blood off my arm, pants, and clothes at least once per week, my mom decided to take matters into her own hands. She made an appointment for me to go to the doctor so he could get to the root of the problem. He removed my wart. When he did, an amazing thing happened: I never had a bloody elbow again.

Here's how this applies to the situation you're in right now. If you're ever to stop "going too far," you have to get to the root of the problem. You have to take matters into your own hands and have some warts removed.

Here are some ways to remove the problem.

1. End the Relationship

The first, and most obvious, way to remove the problem of going too far is to end the relationship. I know this is tough to do, and I'm not saying it has to be 100 percent permanent. However, even if you both have said you're sorry and promised it won't happen again, it is way too fresh in both of your minds. If you put yourselves in the same situation, you will fall again, just as you did last time. Therefore, you need to take a break. End the relationship, and give it several months before you even think about getting back together.

2. Plan Out Date Night Details

The second way to remove the problem of going too far is to plan out all the details of your date night. What are you doing? Where are you going? What time are you leaving? When are you getting back? Who will be with you? These are all questions you need definite answers to every time you go out on a date, because the bottom line is this: If you don't know what you'll do on the date, there's a good chance you and your date might end up compromising.

3. Stop Dating for a While

The third way to remove the problem of going too far is to stop dating for a while. I had a friend one time who had so many speeding tickets and traffic violations that his driver's license got taken away for a while. If you have a track record of going too far too fast physically when you are dating, maybe you need to revoke your own dating license and stop dating, at least for a little while. Take a few months to get yourself emotionally, physically, and spiritually strong before you jump back behind the dating wheel again.

4. Stay Away From Hot Spots

The fourth way to remove the problem of going too far is to stay away from hot spots. When it comes to removing the problem, you've got to stay away from the hot spots where the physical action usually occurs. Here are a few hot spots to stay away from.

Hot Spot #1—Alone at the House

If you drop your date off at ten o'clock and his or her parents won't be back till eleven, let me give you a great piece of advice: Walk to the door together and say good-bye; then you walk back to your car, get back in, and drive home. You and your special someone alone in the house only spells trouble.

Hot Spot #2—Movie Night at the House

Grabbing some movies, heading back to the house, sitting on the couch, and sharing some popcorn while watching a sweet chick flick sounds innocent—and it can be. However, movie night at the house is pretty risky; if not handled properly, this can be a real hot spot.

Hot Spot #3—Bedrooms

Enough said.

Hot Spot #4—Snuggling

Ladies, I'll let you in on a little secret. When your body, your legs, and your arms are all wrapped around and intertwined with your boyfriend's, as you lie together under a blanket on the couch, the entire time you're enjoying snuggling with him, there's a word at the very forefront of his mind that starts with an "s". But rest assured, the word he's thinking about isn't "snuggling".

Restore Your Relationship With God

You've repented of your sin, rejected the guilt, stopped thinking and talking about it, and removed the problem. Now it's time to restore your relationship with God.

One of the things I love about the Bible is its brutal honesty. The heroes of Scripture were anything but perfect. Moses killed a man in cold blood. (Ex. 2.) Abraham was a chronic liar. (Gen. 20:2-7.) David had a serious lust problem. (2 Sam. 11.) Zacchaeus, the wee little tax collector, was a thief. (Luke 19:8.) Peter denied Jesus. (Luke 22.) James and John were hot-heads, and Thomas had some big-time faith issues. (John 20.) However, when you look at their lives with all of their shortcomings, they all—each and every one of them—restored their personal relationship with God and went on to experience the amazing lives He planned for them.

It's the same with you. When you're brutally honest with yourself, you know you're not perfect. You've made some mistakes. But just like Peter, James, Moses, and a short little guy named Zacchaeus, you can restore your relationship with God.

If you will not just read the things I've talked about in this chapter but actually begin to do them, your relationship with God—in spite of anything you may have messed up in—will be restored.

If You've Gone Too Far

Let's recap really quickly. What do you do when you've gone too far? First, repent of your sin. Simply come to God and repent of the sin you committed, and He will forgive you. Second, reject the guilt. Don't carry around the excess baggage of guilt. Put the past where it belongs: behind you. Third, remove the problem. Do whatever you have to do to not put yourself in a situation to fall again. The price Jesus paid is way too high, and the life you can have in Him is way too good to throw it all away by putting yourself in situations in which you know you could fail sexually—so stay away from the hot spots.

Finally, restore your relationship with God. He loves you, and the most important thing to Him is that you come to Him. He will restore you when you do.

What Do I
Do When...

I've Been
Dumped?

Getting dumped stinks for a whole lot of reasons, doesn't it?

First of all, you don't want other people to make decisions for you. You want to control your own destiny; and if the relationship needed to end, then you should have been the one to end it. Right? It's just not right when the person who walks up and says, "It's over," isn't you.

Secondly, you really liked this person. You were thinking everything was going pretty well. Maybe not perfectly, but whose relationship is perfect? Anyway, things were tracking along pretty well when all of a sudden out of nowhere—it's done. And now you're faced with trying to figure out why.

Also, depending on how much your friends knew how you felt about this person, getting dumped can be pretty awkward. The day after it all went down, you have to answer questions and talk about it with everyone. As you walk to class, you feel the stares of people watching you, and you can't help but wonder what they're thinking or saying.

Getting dumped...stinks.

If you've recently felt the pain of someone you cared about "letting you go," here are some things you need to do.

Trust God

If you're experiencing the pain of being dumped, the first thing you need to learn to do is to trust God. I know that's easier said than done. A lot of people have trust issues, and I think I know the reason why.

Do you remember going to the swimming pool when you were a little kid? You stood there in your Barney swim trunks or Barbie swimsuit playing and having fun on the side of the pool when your dad came up to you and said, "Jump in the pool. I'll catch you!"

He started to walk closer to the side of the pool, you stepped a little closer to the edge, and your dad raised his arms and said, "Go ahead! Jump! I'll catch you." You were scared to death, but you scooted a little closer to the edge. Your dad smiled and said, "Trust me. I'll catch you. I promise. Go ahead and jump!"

You were thinking, *He's my dad. He wouldn't lie,* so you took a deep breath and jumped. And just as he promised, he was right there to catch you. You smiled and laughed. It was actually pretty fun, so you went right back to the edge of the pool and jumped again and again. Each time you jumped, your dad promised to catch you; and each time you jumped, he came through.

After about five or six jumps, you totally trusted your father and jumped into his arms without thinking about it.

Then it happened. Your dad once again said, "Jump. I'll catch you." You closed your eyes and jumped but this time, instead of feeling your father's arms wrapping around you as they had so many times before, this time you felt yourself splash into the water. You were all alone, sinking toward the bottom. He was standing right there, but he didn't catch you. He lied. Your dad lied, and even though you were fine and by no means had your dad meant to harm you, it was from that time on that you began to realize people don't always come through on their promises.

Many people have trust issues, and when they hear things like "Trust God," they feel like a little kid standing on the side of the pool hearing their father say, "Jump. I promise I'll catch you." Even though they want to, it's hard to trust people they can see, let alone put their lives into the hands of Someone they can't.

Many people have trust issues. Because of your recent breakup, you may be one of these people. Like a kid jumping off the side of a pool, you thought things would continue on as they always had. But now that the relationship is over, you feel all alone and like you're sinking emotionally to the bottom of the pool.

I know it may be hard, but the first thing you need to do after a breakup is trust God. I know you've probably trusted other people and been let down before, but that is exactly why you need to trust God. God is the only thing in your life that never, ever fails. Scriptures tell us that "God is not a man that he should lie; nor a son of man, that he should change his mind.

Does he speak and then not act? Does he promise and then not fulfill?" (Num. 23:19). When God says something, you can count on it.

God's Promises To You

I want you to look at some of the promises God has made to you.

Proverbs 3:5-6 says, "Trust in the LORD with all your heart and lean not on your own understanding; in all your ways acknowledge him, and he will make your paths straight."

As a child of God, you have to make the decision to trust your Father. Other people may have let you down, but He won't. If you'll simply make the decision to trust God's plan for your life by acknowledging Him in all your ways, including your dating life, God—your heavenly Father—promises to make sure you end up all right in the end.

Proverbs 16:9 says, "In his heart a man plans his course, but the LORD determines his steps."

Most likely, you had some plans for the relationship you were in. You liked this person, and this person liked you. You could see this thing going somewhere.

That's fine. In fact, it's good to make plans and have dreams for your life. However, you need to understand that God has the roadmap of your life all planned out. He sees the big picture, and He loves you so much He is moving your life around in order for you to achieve His plan for you. So trust Him. I know it hurts right now, but rest assured that God has your back. He will not lead you down the wrong path.

Deuteronomy 31:6 says, "Be strong and courageous. Do not be afraid or terrified because of them, for the LORD your God goes with you; he will never leave you nor forsake you."

Okay, you've probably had a lot of people come and go in your life, and this latest breakup is just one of several. It's easy for us to think God is just like the other people we have relationships with in our lives. We think He will come and He will go; He'll be here for a while, and then He'll be gone.

However, that is the furthest thing from the truth. The truth of the matter is, on the day you were born, God was there. On your first day of school, God was there. That Christmas when you were jumping all around your living room because you got the present you were wanting, God was right there jumping with you. When you had your first crush, God was there. And a few days ago when it all went down, God was there, as well.

God has been and always will be with you. Other people will come and go in your life, but God is not one of them. He is the single and solitary constant in your life. Let Him be your guide through this situation. He promised that He would, so trust Him.

Don't Let Others Determine Your Self-Worth

The second thing you need to do when someone has let you down is to not let others determine your self-worth. One thing I hate to do is go to garage sales. Some people like rummaging through a bunch of stuff that other people no longer have a use for. To them, there is nothing better than spending a Saturday morning driving through the neighborhood trying to find a great deal on an old toaster or a sweet lampshade. Some people love garage sales. I, however, am not one of those people.

One of the reasons I don't like garage sales is that it is depressing. Every time I go to a garage sale, it hits me that I'm looking through piles of items that some family once wanted but now has no use for so they're trying to pawn it off on me for 50 cents. Garage sale items used to be valuable, but now they're of little or no value at all.

When you get dumped, it's easy to feel like a garage sale item. At one time, you were valuable and the person couldn't live without you. But now you've been thrown out like an old Nintendo 64 game system, and it hurts. Even though things didn't work out between you two, you need to know you're not a garage sale item whose value it is determined by its previous owner. No, you're much more valuable than that.

Psalm 139:14 says, "I praise you because I am fearfully and wonderfully made; your works are wonderful, I know that full well." Scripture says you're fearfully and wonderfully made. The thing that determines your value is the One who created you.

Think about it for a minute. If I had a one hundred dollar bill, would you want it? Sure, you would. Right? What if I stepped on it? Would you still want it? Sure, you would. What if I rolled it up in a ball? Would you still want it? Sure, you would. What if I spit on it and then drove my car over it? Would you still want it? Sure, you would.

But why would you want it? It's been rolled up, stepped on, spit on, and driven over. Why would you still want this beat-up and used one hundred dollar bill? You would want it because it's worth one hundred dollars. Right?

The things that have been done to it don't determine its value. You see, a one hundred dollar bill is worth one hundred dollars because the U.S. government (its creator) says it's worth one hundred dollars—not because of its circumstances.

It's the exact same way with you. You may have been emotionally hurt; you may have been called some harsh things that made you feel like a second-class garage sale item. However, what's happened to you doesn't set your value; the One who created you does.

He says you are fearfully and wonderfully made. You have an inherent value given to you by your Creator that can never be taken away.

So the next time you think about yourself or look in the mirror, don't let what someone else has said or done be the determining factor on your value. Let God, your Creator, show you how much you're really worth.

Don't Jump Right Into Another Relationship

When someone's broken up with you, the third thing you need to do is to avoid a rebound relationship. It happens all the time. You go through a tough breakup. Someone's there to pick up the pieces, and it just so happens that someone is cute. So you start spending time with this hottie. You let each other know how you feel, and before you know it, you're going out. Within a few short weeks, the emotions wear off, one thing leads to another, and you go through another tough break up. Again, someone is there to pick up the pieces. It just so happens that someone is cute, and the cycle begins all over again.

When you've gone through a breakup, don't jump right back into another relationship. Take a time-out and catch your breath before you jump right back into the dating game.

Proverbs 21:5 says, "The plans of the diligent lead to profit as surely as haste leads to poverty." When was the last time you did something—anything—on a whim and it actually worked out well? Remember that pair of jeans, that hat, or the paint-ball gun you just had to have? How did that work out? Or what about the time you decided to not study for the test but to just "wing it"? How did that work out for you? Most likely not too well. Right?

Anytime you do something hastily, you'll most likely regret it. So let me ask you a question. You just went through a break up... what are your plans now? What do you want to do? Where will you go? What are a few things you need to improve on? What's coming up next for you? Why is this next person so much different from the last?

Until you can answer some of these questions, you don't need to get involved again in a relationship.

In fact, God warns us in 1 Timothy 5:22, "Do not be hasty in the laying on of hands, and do not share in the sins of others. Keep yourself pure." Invariably, you make bad decisions and then have to live with the negative ramifications and conse-quences of those decisions when you bring someone into your personal life too quickly.

Let me ask you a question. What would it hurt you to take a little break from the dating carousel? What really bad thing would happen if you jumped off for a little while and began to work on who you are rather than who you want?

Don't get caught in the *start dating, break up, start dating, break up again* cycle. Don't jump right back into another relationship.

Things To Do Instead of Dating

Here are few things you could do rather than date.

1. ### Focus on Education

    First, you can focus on education. I know doing home-work probably pales in comparison to going out with someone who gives you the tingles in your tummy. However, here's something someone once told me. The more you learn, the more you'll earn. The more you earn, the more fun you can have when it's time to get down to some serious dating. So while you're on your dating sab-batical...learn something.

2. ### Start a New Hobby

    Second, rather than thinking about dating, try starting a new hobby. What is it that you have always wanted to do, learn or experience? You have some free time on your hands, so what is stopping you? Take an art class, go out for a new sport, get some computer software and master graphic design. Again, knowing who you are is going to determine what you want, so take a few months to discover some of your hidden talents.

3. Hang Out With Your Friends

Third, to get your mind off of dating for a awhile, hang out with your friends. What are you doing this weekend? Probably nothing, so text a few of your buds and have them over to your house for the weekend. Start up a huge *Halo 3* tournament, go shopping, have a movie night, go paintballing, go to a ball game, or just go to the mall and hang out. I'm sure that while you were dating there were times you wanted to hang out with your friends. Now is a great time.

4. Get Better at What You're Good At

Fourth, to get your mind off dating, focus on getting better at what you're good at. What are you good at? Think about it for a minute. What's something you think you could become great at if you really put time, energy, and effort into it? Instead of taking the next few weeks and months looking for and investing time in someone else, why not take some time to invest in you? Take something you are good at, and become great.

Onto Better Things

If you've been dumped, trust God, don't let others determine your self-worth, and don't jump into another relationship. This is not the time for you to focus all of your time and effort on someone else. This is the time for you to focus on who you are and the potential God has put inside you. Remember: God is with you every step of the way, and you will get through this pain and onto bigger and better things!

What Do I
Do When...

I Know
I Need
To End the
Relationship?

I love amusement parks. I can't get enough of roller coaster rides. My favorite roller coaster of all time is the Magnum XL-2000 at Cedar Point in Sandusky, Ohio. This ride is absolutely sick. It has some nasty hills, unbelievable drops, and tops off at like sixty-eight miles per hour. It's not the tallest or fastest coaster out there, but the ride as a whole is unbelievable!

The thing about the Magnum XL-2000 is that the ride lasts about two and a half minutes and then it's over. When the ride comes to a stop, it's time to stand up, get out of the car, and move on.

The same can be said for dating. Dating is an amazing ride full of emotional ups and downs. There's really nothing quite like it. However, just like the great Magnum XL-2000, all rides must come to an end. Unless you get married (and statistically, chances are you won't), there will come a time when the fun is over and you need to stand up, get out of the relationship, and move on. When that time comes, here are a few things you need to do.

Be Honest With Yourself

When it's time to break up with someone, the first thing you have to do is be honest with yourself.

You started going out a little while ago. At first, things were going well. In fact, they were going great. But now it's a little different. You're not as into this person anymore. You don't have a whole lot in common, and you're pretty sure it's over.

If that's the case, be honest with yourself. Nothing good will come out of trying to prop up your relationship to keep it going. In fact, in a dating relationship, that can be very dangerous. You'll try to keep it going by getting more involved emotionally and physically, and when the breakup does happen, which it will, you'll be left with even more pain and regret than if you would have ended it months before.

If the relationship is over and you want to move on, be honest with yourself.

Be Honest With the Other Person

When it's time to break up with someone, the second thing you have to do is be honest with the other person. Don't beat around the bush. Don't lie. Just be honest. If you're crushing on someone else, be honest and admit it. If you're just ready to stop dating and focus on yourself, be honest about it. If you like the person a lot but things are going a little too fast and you need to take a break, be honest.

Telling your date some stupid made-up lie is not only rude, but it makes no sense because eventually the truth will get back around to the person and then (depending on the real reason for the breakup), you'll look like the bad guy.

There's no reason to keep things going if it's time to end them, and there's no reason to do anything other than look the person in the eye and tell the truth.

Follow the Golden Rule

When it's time to break up with someone, the third thing you need to do is follow the Golden Rule. This is a really good rule to live your life by, and it goes something like this. "Do to others as you would have them do to you" (Luke 6:31). This rule was spoken by a pretty smart guy (Jesus), so it may be something you want to do when it comes to your breakup.

1. During the Breakup

   During a breakup, follow the Golden Rule. Treat the other person the way you would want to be treated.

   Would you want to find out your dating relationship is over by some kid coming up and telling you, "Hey, [*insert your date's name here*] wants you to know it's over"? No? So don't do that to your date.

   Would you think it was classy if your date sent you a text message with these three words: "It's over, loser"? No? Then don't break up with your date like that.

Would you be fine if you just started getting the silent treatment from the person you cared about, until one day you were forced to ask what's going on? No? Then don't do that to your date.

When you're going to break up with someone, do it with some class. This is someone you care—or at least *cared*—about, so break it off the way you would want someone to break up with you. Look the person in the eye and talk one on one; your date deserves that decency.

2. After the Breakup

After the breakup has gone down, the Golden Rule still applies. Treat your ex the way you would like to be treated.

You wouldn't like it if you got some wicked text messages, got the cold shoulder, or heard a bunch of rumors flying around about you—so don't do those things to your ex. In fact, it may seem awkward or weird, but if at all possible try your best to still be friends.

If Possible, Still Be Friends

Who says breakups have to be nasty and, after they're over, you have to go your separate ways and never speak again? The truth of the matter is that this is someone you probably had a lot of fun with, laughed with, had some things in common with, and maybe even shared some secrets with. You don't have to cut this person off and out of your life.

If possible, still be friends. When you see this person, say hello. If you're hanging out at the game and he or she walks up, go ahead and talk.

This can take on a lot of different shapes, but unless your ex was a 100 percent jerkball, treat him or her the way you would like to be treated and still be friends.

What Do I
Do When...

I Want to Set
    Personal
Boundaries?

These next few years of your life are going to be amazing. You're going to be overwhelmed with emotions and experiences that you'll never be able to capture again. My advice is this: enjoy it!

However, when you're figuring out who you will and will not go out with, and where you should draw the magic line of "too far," here are a few things you need to remember.

The Big Difference Between Love and Lust

To determine where your boundary line will be, the first thing you need to do is remember there's a big difference between love and lust. In fact, the only thing love and lust have in common is that they both start with the letter *L*. That's it. Love is all about the other person, and lust is all about you. Take a look at what the Bible says about each of these powerful *L*-words.

1. Love

   If I speak in the tongues of men and of angels, but have not love, I am only a resounding gong or a clanging cymbal. If I have the gift of prophecy and can fathom all mysteries and all knowledge, and if I have a faith that can move mountains, but have not love, I am nothing. If I give all I possess to the poor and surrender my body to the flames, but have not love, I gain nothing.

Love is patient, love is kind. It does not envy, it does not boast, it is not proud. It is not rude, it is not self-seeking, it is not easily angered, it keeps no record of wrongs. Love does not delight in evil but rejoices with the truth. It always protects, always trusts, always hopes, always perseveres.

Love never fails.

1 Corinthians 13:1-8

2. Lust

I made a covenant with my eyes not to look lustfully at a girl.

Job 31:1

Do not lust in your heart after her beauty or let her captivate you with her eyes.

Proverbs 6:25

Put to death, therefore, whatever belongs to your earthly nature: sexual immorality, impurity, lust, evil desires and greed, which is idolatry.

Colossians 3:5

But I tell you that anyone who looks at a woman lustfully has already committed adultery with her in his heart.

Matthew 5:28

As you can see, God looks at love and lust as two entirely different things. You should, too. When getting to know someone, make sure you're cultivating *love* and not *lust*.

What You Do With Your Body Is Very Important

In setting your personal boundary lines, the second thing you need to remember is that what you do with your body is very important. A lot of people think, *Hey, it's my body; I'll do what I want with it.* I guess that's true to some extent. However, your body, though you live in it, actually belongs to God. So you need to be very careful what you do with and how you use your body, especially when it comes to sexual things. Here's what the Scriptures have to say about your body.

> In the same way, count yourselves dead to sin but alive to God in Christ Jesus. Therefore do not let sin reign in your mortal body so that you obey its evil desires. Do not offer the parts of your body to sin, as instruments of wickedness, but rather offer yourselves to God, as those who have been brought from death to life; and offer the parts of your body to him as instruments of righteousness.
>
> Romans 6:11-13

> Don't you know that when you offer yourselves to someone to obey him as slaves, you are slaves to the

one whom you obey—whether you are slaves to sin, which leads to death, or to obedience, which leads to righteousness? But thanks be to God that, though you used to be slaves to sin, you wholeheartedly obeyed the form of teaching to which you were entrusted. You have been set free from sin and have become slaves to righteousness.

Romans 6:16-18

Therefore, I urge you, brothers, in view of God's mercy, to offer your bodies as living sacrifices, holy and pleasing to God—this is your spiritual act of worship.

Romans 12:1

If You're a Christian, Then Date Christians

The third thing you need to remember when setting your personal boundary lines is that if you're a Christian, then you need to be dating other Christians. This is a huge hang-up for a lot of people. I've had a lot of people through the years say, "Date only Christians? How is that possible? I don't know any cute Christians. Besides, I'll stay right with God. I'm not going to compromise my faith."

To that, I always reply with this Scripture:

> Do not be yoked together with unbelievers. For what
> do righteousness and wickedness have in common?
> Or what fellowship can light have with darkness?

2 Corinthians 6:14

You see, God through His Word has set His standard for you as His child. He says that you should not be "yoked"—or closely tied to—a person who is not right with Him. This is His standard. When you go out with someone who isn't right with God, you have already compromised God's standard. If you have compromised once, the next compromise is right around the corner. So date only believers.

Sex Is for Marriage Only

The fourth thing you need to remember when setting your personal boundary lines is that sex is for marriage only. Hebrews 13:4 says, "Marriage should be honored by all, and the marriage bed kept pure, for God will judge the adulterer and all the sexually immoral."

What happens between a married man and woman in their bed is a wonderful and pure thing in God's eyes. However, when those same things happen between two people who aren't married, it breaks God's heart. Scripture teaches us that's sin and will be judged.

So here's the thing. Go out, date, and have a great time. But save the physical stuff for the right time—when you are married. You and your future husband or wife will be so glad you did!

Conclusion

We've all got so many questions about sex, love, and dating. I hope this book has answered some of yours. We've tackled what to do when your parents won't let you date, when someone doesn't even know you exist, when you're going on your first date, when you think you're in love, when your date wants to get physical, when you've gone too far, when you've been dumped, when you need to dump someone, and when you want to set some boundaries.

Whether you're waiting to enter the dating game, you're in a great relationship, or you're in the middle of a painful breakup, I want to encourage you that you have a great life ahead of you. God wants to be with you every step of the way, and I pray you'll draw close to Him during this very exciting, though sometimes painful, time of your life. Trust Him, and His promise is that He will direct your path. With that promise, you can be sure you have a fantastic journey ahead. Follow Him in your relationships, and you can't go wrong!

Prayer of Salvation

God loves you—no matter who you are, no matter what your past. God loves you so much that He gave His one and only begotten Son for you. The Bible tells us that "…whoever believes in him shall not perish but have eternal life" (John 3:16). Jesus laid down His life and rose again so that we could spend eternity with Him in heaven and experience His absolute best on earth. If you would like to receive Jesus into your life, say the following prayer out loud and mean it from your heart.

Heavenly Father, I come to You admitting that I am a sinner. Right now, I choose to turn away from sin, and I ask You to cleanse me of all unrighteousness. I believe that Your Son, Jesus, died on the cross to take away my sins. I also believe that He rose again from the dead so that I might be forgiven of my sins and made righteous through faith in Him. I call upon the name of Jesus Christ to be the Savior and Lord of my life. Jesus, I choose to follow You and ask that You fill me with the power of the Holy Spirit. I declare that right now I am a child of God. I am free from sin and full of the righteousness of God. I am saved in Jesus' name. Amen.

If you prayed this prayer to receive Jesus Christ as your Savior for the first time, please contact us on the web at **www.harrisonhouse.com** to receive a free book.

Or you may write to us at

Harrison House

P.O. Box 35035

Tulsa, Oklahoma 74153

About Kevin Moore

Kevin Moore is the youth pastor of Oneighty® the youth ministry of Church on the Move in Tulsa, Oklahoma. With more than 16 years experience in youth ministry, Kevin's passion in life is to introduce teenagers to the person of Jesus Christ and help them walk out their faith in a real and personal way.

Throughout the year Kevin travels and speaks at leadership and student conferences around nation. The biblical principles he shares are proven to work in any size church or city.

Kevin and his wife Veronica have been married for 17 years. They have four children: Jordan 16, Logan 13, Mikayla 9, and Lilly Grace, 1 year old.

You can contact Kevin Moore at
growmoore@gmail.com
www.twitter.com/kevinmoore180
www.facebook.com/kevinmoore180
P.O. Box 692032
Tulsa, OK 74169-2032

Read Kevin's blog at www.kevinmoore.tumblr.com

Please include your prayer requests
and comments when you write.

Other Books in the
What Do I Do When? Series

What Do I Do When—Answering Your
Toughest Questions About God

Kevin Moore encourages you to seek God for yourself in
the Scriptures and in your own heart, plus answers questions like: "Why do bad things happen to good people?"
and "What do I do when I'm a Christian but the feelings
are gone?" You will discover amazing things about God

and learn a lot about yourself along
the way.

What Do I Do When?

*Answering Your Toughest
Questions About God*

978-1-57794-959-6

What Do I Do When...Money

Moore counsels you that you cannot identify yourself by
what you have, that loving money is a big mistake, and
what you can do to guard your heart against greed. You
will gain a great foundation to build your future on, putting

God first and using money as a
tool to achieve your dreams.

What Do I Do When?

*Answering Your Toughest
Questions About Money*

978-1-57794-960-2

What Do I Do When—Answering Your Toughest Questions About Friends

Filled with humor and grounded in God's Word, Moore answers your tough questions about friends including: "What do I do when my friends don't want Jesus?" and "What do I do when my friend is mean?" You will be empowered to act in love and common sense with

Moore's comical, yet strong, biblical advice.

What Do I Do When?

Answering Your Toughest Questions About Friends

978-1-57794-962-6

The Harrison House Vision

Proclaiming the truth and the power

Of the Gospel of Jesus Christ

With excellence;

Challenging Christians to

Live victoriously,

Grow spiritually,

Know God intimately.